Play the game:

Soccer

THE FOOTBALL ASSOCIATION
and
THE NATIONAL COACHING FOUNDATION

ISBN 0 947850 55 4

First published 1988 by
The Football Association, Education and
Coaching Department, 16 Lancaster Gate,
London W2 3LW
and **The National Coaching Foundation**,
4 College Close, Beckett Park, Leeds
LS6 3QH

Designed and produced by
White Line Press, 60 Bradford Road,
Stanningley, Leeds LS28 6EF
for the Publishers

Illustrations: Steve McGarry
Design: Krystyna Hewitt
Typeset in 10/10½ pt Franklin Gothic Book
by Jill Tempest Phototypesetting
Printed and bound in Great Britain

Acknowledgements

The Football Association gratefully
acknowledges the time and effort
contributed by the National Coaching
Foundation and the Sports Council to the
production of this publication, and the
financial help received from the Football
Trust.

Play the Game of Soccer is a revised,
updated and extended version of *Play the
Game*, first published by the National
Coaching Foundation and Play Board, and
based on *Fair Play Codes for Children in
Sport* (Task Force of the Canadian Council
on Children and Youth).

Contents

Foreword

**By His Royal Highness the Duke of Kent
President of the Football Association**

The history of Association Football is really the story of a game which has brought enormous enjoyment to countless millions of people all over the world for more than a hundred years.

To a great extent, enjoyment has not been in the winning but in taking part, be it as a player, spectator, teacher, referee, administrator or commentator.

In more recent times, the enjoyment of the majority has been spoiled by the inconsiderate behaviour of the few. On some occasions, players at all levels have placed an unhealthy importance on winning, while at other times spectators have allowed partisan support to develop into something closely resembling tribal warfare.

I believe that The Football Association and its affiliated membership must now make a concerted effort to place a greater emphasis on sportsmanship and to re-establish higher standards of behaviour amongst all its participants.

Association Football occupies an important place in our national life, and as such it should be a force for good. This booklet, *Play the Game of Soccer*, is designed to help all those concerned with the training of young footballers to appreciate that there is more to the enjoyment of football than winning at any cost, and so enable them to develop young players into sportsmen and sportswomen.

I hope this booklet will be widely read and that it may prove to be the catalyst which leads to improved standards of behaviour both on and off the field.

Just as a teacher should accept responsibility for the behaviour of the children in the class during a lesson, so the manager, or coach, of a football team must accept responsibility for the behaviour of the players in the team during a game.

If children misbehave at home it reflects badly on the parents; if children misbehave at school it reflects badly on the teachers; and if players misbehave on the football field it reflects badly on the managers and coaches.

The improvement of the behaviour of players on the field, therefore, lies in the hands of managers and coaches.

I want all of you who coach and manage teams to join me in helping to improve behaviour on the field. The first step in that process is to accept that the behaviour of players on the field is our responsibility. I want you also to know that every player in every England Squad is made fully aware that their behaviour is under the microscope, and that I expect the standard of behaviour which we would all be pleased for young players to emulate.

This booklet will be helpful to you. Please read it carefully and translate these principles into practice.

Bobby Robson

Introduction

What can soccer offer children and young people?

Soccer has a great deal to offer children and young people. Apart from the joy of physical activity in itself, it gives them the chance to develop a sense of self-worth, a knowledge of their own abilities, an opportunity to work in co-operation with others and an understanding of competition. Soccer allows children to experiment physically and emotionally in a healthy and safe environment. In short, it gives children and young people the chance to develop some of the skills needed for everyday life.

Through soccer, youngsters can develop an enthusiasm for active participation which can become the basis of a healthy and active lifestyle.

And yet . . .

A child's happy participation in soccer will be put at risk if the adults involved have the wrong attitudes. For example, play is an essential part of a child's development, yet some adults have a tendency to forget this in their emphasis on winning at all costs. There are dangers in forcing children beyond their capabilities and differing levels of interest.

There is a need for tremendous patience while the child develops his or her own sense of direction and purpose, and the body develops its own strengths and capabilities. Competition can be of great value in providing the needed edge, the challenge to strive for a personal goal, but competition should be used to highlight and develop personal performance, not merely to measure it. The attitude that players should win at all costs must be avoided.

This booklet has been developed to assist everybody who helps young people play soccer. The guidelines provided will help you to be a positive influence in the development of the youngsters in your charge.

Where is the "play" in sport?

Over the past few decades some alarming trends have appeared in children's sport in general and soccer in particular:
- the stress on winning at all costs
- the increasing amount of violence
- the undue pressure on youngsters for higher achievement
- more and more demanding competitions and training programmes

These trends reflect adult sport and stem in part from the idea that children's sport is merely a scaled down version of the adult world — **a false and dangerous idea**. However, there are some welcome signs of a change in this outlook.

Do remember . . .

Children should play as children, not as small adults. The media show professional sport at its best . . . and its worst. It is up to adults to ensure that the influence on children is positive and helpful. Adults can help children watching "grown up" and professional sports to find values and role-models, and to copy high levels of skill. They can help children to maintain a sense of perspective and proportion.

Most importantly, adults must ensure that they themselves have realistic expectations of children in sport, which means being aware of the needs and characteristics of growing children. Soccer is enjoyable for the game itself, but it is also about:
- discipline, persistence and teamwork
- developing a sense of self-esteem, of personal limits and potential
- discovery, experimentation, fun, free expression and play chosen by children themselves
- achievement of the best possible results

Setting high personal standards – by always keeping kit clean, for example – can help to develop a sense of self-esteem

Having the right attitude towards winning enables you to recognise the success of others

Keeping the fun in soccer can be extremely hard. Merely measuring the value of soccer by whether a child can win or not, score or not, defeat or be defeated, will not do it. It is better to stress the development of a sense of personal worth and achievement.

What happens to children or young people when they lose?

Unless a sense of satisfaction can be developed simply from having taken part, tried hard and overcome personal obstacles, more and more performers are going to suffer. Frustrated by the constant pressure to win, they will drop out because they feel inadequate or inferior.

There is another way of defining competition and winning — a way which will relieve some of the strains before they begin.

What is needed is a new view of competition which emphasises the rewards:

• of trying to do better than last time

• of persistence

• of setting one's own goals and finding the discipline to have a go at them

• of co-operation in playing for the team

• of sheer athletic joy

When winning is kept in perspective, there is room for fun in the pursuit of victory — or, more accurately, the pursuit of victory **is fun**. It is up to you to help children see competition this way.

We are not suggesting that winning is unimportant — just that it is not the **most** important thing.

What is excellence?

There have been many attempts to define "excellence" and fit it to groups of performers, but the concept has often been used in a very limited way. This has led to a misunderstanding of the idea of excellence and a mistrust of the methods of achieving it, particularly with young performers. **Everyone** can achieve excellence — it is a matter of attitude and intention rather than simply being high in the league.

Only a few will reach the standards set by players such as Charlton, Pelé or Johann Cruyff, but this should not stop the rest of us attempting to achieve our own personal excellence. Through persistence, hard work and dedication, every player can **achieve** and be **successful**. The challenge for the adults involved in soccer is to help each child set his/her own realistic goals and to provide support while he/she strives to achieve them.

Soccer for youngsters — the issues

The major problems in children's soccer can be summarised:

• the "win at all costs" approach, leading to physical and mental stress and resulting in a lack of enjoyment

• a lack of knowledge on the part of coaches and parents about children's growth and development, so that they place unrealistic expectations on the child

• use of adult values and rules, distorting the child's approach to participation

• lack of respect for the abilities and skills of others, resulting in conflict

• a lack of sportsmanship in some areas

• violence, and the tendency of the media to highlight violence and rough play

Violence and threats destroy sportsmanship and spoil the game for others

Soccer — play the game

To deal with these problems, it is necessary to return to a situation where the child is at the centre of things. This will allow the quality of play to be improved, and will meet the needs of all young sport participants whatever their abilities and skills. The "Play the Game" guidelines which follow are designed to reinforce the positive elements of children's participation in soccer. The guidelines are designed:

• to ensure that children and young people find enjoyment and lasting satisfaction through participating in physical activity, especially soccer

• to make adults aware that children play to satisfy themselves, and not necessarily to satisfy adults and their ambitions

• to encourage children and young people to become fit and healthy by making soccer attractive, safe and enjoyable

Everybody has a responsibility to "play the game" — players, coaches, officials, parents, administrators and spectators. Together their attitudes and actions can ensure high standards of sporting behaviour and help to emphasise fun, friendly competition and individual fulfilment.

Coaches/Team Managers

The successful coach[1] is concerned more in the well-being and interests of the players than in his/her win-loss record.

• be reasonable in your demands on children's and young people's time, energy and enthusiasm — they need other interests too

• children play for fun and enjoyment, and winning is only part of this. Never ridicule of shout at the children for making mistakes or losing a competition

• make a personal commitment to keep yourself informed on sound coaching principles and the principles of children's growth and development. The addresses given on page 17 will help

• group your players according to age, height, skill and physical maturity where appropriate

• the length of practices and competitions should take into consideration the maturity of thc children

• avoid over-playing the talented players. The "just-average" players need and deserve equal time. **Be sensitive to the less talented**

• ensure that equipment and facilities meet safety standards and are appropriate to the age and ability of the players

• follow the advice of a medically qualified person when deciding when an injured player is ready to play again

• teach your players that the rules of the game are mutual agreements which no one should break

• develop respect for the ability of opponents, as well as for the judgement of officials and opposing coaches

• don't publicly question any official's decisions, and never doubt his or her honesty.

[1]Note: You may call yourself a coach or a team manager. No matter. When we use the word *coach* in this booklet, it refers to you whatever is your title.

You play an important role in youth soccer. You teach the skills of the sport and promote fitness. You also become an important person in the young athlete's life, and can have an influence on his/her personal and social development. Likewise, the involvement of parents in soccer programmes can bring families closer together and heighten the value of the sport experience.

The "soccer triangle", consisting of child, coach and parent, is a natural aspect of youth sport, so your role in dealing with parents is very important to the success of the programme. Through their co-operation many parents contribute to

The "soccer triangle"

sport. Some, through lack of understanding, can undermine youth sport and deprive children of many benefits. As a coach, you should be able to channel parents' genuine concerns and good intentions in a way that supports what you are trying to accomplish.

Parents have a right to know what is happening to their child, so you should be willing to answer their questions. Remember that communication is two-way: if you keep the lines open, your relations with parents will be more likely to be constructive and enjoyable.

Fostering two-way communication does not mean that parents are free to be disrespectful toward you. Rather, it is an open invitation for parents to express their concerns with the assurance that you will listen to them. There is, however, a proper time for them to discuss things with you. That time is never during a practice or a game, and only rarely when the children are there!

The most common cause of problems between coaches and parents is differences of opinion about the young players' abilities. Sometimes parents will disagree with what you are doing. The main thing is not to get defensive. Listen to what they have to say. You might find some of the suggestions helpful. But even if you do not agree, you can at least afford to listen politely. Realise that you, as coach, have the final say. Remember that no coach can please everyone. The key is to try your best — nobody can ask for anything more than that.

Parents

Children, as you know, develop differently and at different rates; they react differently to the same pressures. Remember:
- children should not be forced to participate in soccer; they are not playing to satisfy **your** ambitions
- children and young people are involved in soccer for **their** enjoyment — not yours

- always encourage your child to play by the rules
- teach your child that effort and teamwork are as important as victory, so that the result of each game is accepted without undue disappointment
- never ridicule or shout at your child for making a mistake or losing a competition
- children learn best by example. Applaud good play by your team **and** by members of the opposing team
- don't publicly question any official's decisions, and never doubt his or her honesty
- support all efforts to remove verbal and physical abuse from children's soccer
- recognise the value and importance of coaches. They give their time and efforts to help your child
- set an example by being friendly to the parents of the opposition!
- emphasise enjoyment and fun
- praise effort as well as improvement

Children at play are not professional entertainers.

• Children play organised soccer for their own enjoyment. They are not there to entertain you, and they are neither miniature adults nor professional sportsmen and women

• don't harass or swear at players, coaches or officials

• applaud good play by your own and the opposing team

• show respect for your team's opponents. Without them there would be no game

• never ridicule or scold a child for making a mistake during a competition

• condemn the use of violence in all forms

• respect the officials' decisions

• encourage players always to play by the rules

• relax and enjoy the game whether your team wins or not

Young players

You will get much more out of soccer if you follow these simple guidelines. **How** you play is far more important than winning or losing.

• play for the "fun of it", not just to please your parents or coach

• where rules apply, try to understand them and stick to them

Don't argue with referees or linesmen

• accept officials' decisions, even if you think they are wrong. Remember we all make mistakes

14

Don't try to referee the game yourself by continually appealing

• control your temper at all times

Don't lose your temper and retaliate if an opponent fouls you

• be a good sport. This means appreciating good play whether it is by your team or your opponents

When playing or watching, praise skilful play by both teams

• remember that the aim of the game is to have fun, to improve your skills, to give your best and to feel good

Practise to improve your play – then you can beat your opponents by your skill

- work equally hard for yourself and your team — your team's performance will benefit and so will your own
- treat all players as you would like to be treated. Don't bully or take unfair advantage of any player
- co-operate with your coach, team-mates, opponents and officials — without them you don't have a game

Co-operation is vital – if a free kick is given against you, get back 10 yards quickly

- don't go over the top when your team scores a goal by jumping all over each other in celebration. Just enjoy your achievement.

League officials

If you become a league official, remember that the administrator is a key figure in making sure that the spirit of the game is "Friendship first — competition second". As an official:

- ensure that all children, regardless of race, ability, sex, age or special needs, have equal opportunities to take part in soccer
- do not allow soccer for youngsters to become primarily spectator entertainment
- ensure that equipment and facilities meet safety standards and are appropriate to the maturity of the children playing
- consider the age and ability of the children when drawing up rules and deciding upon the length and number of games to be played

- make sure soccer is played for its own sake. Play down the importance of awards
- distribute a code of conduct for good sporting attitudes and behaviour to spectators, coaches, players, officials, parents and news media
- try to ensure that parents, coaches, sponsors and participants understand **their** authority and **their** responsibility to ensure fair play in soccer
- try to ensure that proper supervision is provided by qualified coaches and officials
- offer courses to improve the standards of coaching and officiating, with emphasis on positive sporting attitudes and the principles of children's growth and development. Your own county Football Association will always be ready to help in this.

The National Coaching Foundation has been established to provide a service for coaches at national and local levels. It provides training programmes, information services, publications, videos and technical data from home and overseas.

Two NCF courses are particularly relevant:

Coaching Children (NCF Level 2 Course)

Children are not the same as adults. This course looks at the particular needs and difficulties that children encounter in sport, and suggests ways for you to help them reach their goals and get more out of taking part. You will find out how their development affects the way in which they learn and perform, and discover how to make all sports easier and more enjoyable for them.

Children and Competitive Sport (NCF Level 3 Course)

A great deal of sports coaching is done with children. Some of them will become senior athletes, while some may only participate for a short period of their lives. This course is designed to help coaches who have an interest in coaching children, or who are responsible for doing so, to understand them and to provide better sports experiences for them. It will allow coaches to learn how children develop and in what ways they differ from adults. Coaches will also learn how to adapt their methods to accommodate children's different abilities and requirements.

For full details of these courses, and other NCF products and coach development services, please contact:

The National Coaching Foundation
4 College Close, Beckett Park, Leeds LS6 3QH

Telephone: Leeds (0532) 744802
Prestel mailbox: 053274480
Telecom Gold mailbox: 76:NCQ002

Play Board

The National Chidren's Play and Recreation Unit is being "hosted" by the Sports Council for a four-year period, to place a central service to children's play on a sound basis from which it might grow towards independence. Working together with the statutory, voluntary and commercial sectors, the Unit aims to enhance the status and visibility of play as a vital part of human development. As a national resourcing agency with a clear play focus and identity, the Unit gives priority to identifying, enabling and disseminating good practice.

An information and advisory service is available, and the Unit can be contacted via The Sports Council, 16 Upper Woburn Place, London WC1H 0QP. Tel: 01-388 1277

The Football Association

The Coca-Cola/Football Association Soccer Star Scheme

The Football Association has developed a new soccer education programme involving exciting tests to help youngsters master the essential soccer skills.

The Scheme will provide an opportunity for all players — boys and girls — of all abilities and ages to challenge themselves in six easily-organised tests.

The tests can be completed indoors or outdoors in an area approximately the size of a school gymnasium. A minimum amount of equipment is required, and a group of twelve players can be tested in one hour.

The Scheme is open to registered examiners, and registration is through a local workshop.

For details of workshops in your area, please:

• write to Bobby Robson at The Soccer Star Office, The Football Association, 22/24A The Broadway, Darkes Lane, Potters Bar, Hertfordshire EN6 2HH

• or ring 0707 50057 (24-hour answering service).

Also available: the *Soccer Star* video and booklet from all good booksellers.

Suggestions for further reading

Rainer Martens (ed.)
Joy and sadness in children's sports
Champaign, Illinois, USA
Human Kinetics, 1982
360 pp.   ISBN 0 931250 15 3   £12.95

An anthology of articles, aimed at all adults involved in children's sport, on the basic issues, competition and the involvement of coaches and parents.

Rainer Martens *et al.*
Coaching young athletes
Champaign, Illinois, USA
Human Kinetics, 1982

200 pp.   ISBN 0 931250 24 2   £9.95

An easy-to-read and often entertaining introduction to coaching, including a chapter on coaching philosophy as well as the psychological, pedagogical, physiological and sports medicine aspects of children in sport.

Mike Sleap
Mini sport: a handbook for teachers and parents
London
Heinemann Educational, 1984 (2nd edition)

210 pp.   ISBN 0 435 86591 9   Out of print

A practical manual which outlines the concept of "mini-sport". This is sport aimed mainly at 7- to 13-year-olds with scaled-down playing areas and equipment and simplified rules. For each of ten sports (badminton, basketball, cricket, hockey, netball, rounders, rugby, soccer, tennis and volleyball) there are sections on the playing area and equipment, rules, practices, proficiency awards, teaching/coaching qualifications, and reference information including addresses and further reading.

Coaching children and young people
A report of the Northern Ireland Conference of Sport 1983, held at Ulster Polytechnic, 30 September — 2 October 1983
Newtown Abbey, Co. Antrim
Northern Ireland Institute of Coaching, 1984

64 pp.   £5.00

(Available from the Northern Ireland Institute of Coaching, Room 15C03, Ulster Polytechnic, Shore Road, Newtown Abbey, County Antrim BT37 0QB.)

Selected conference papers given by distinguished speakers (including Rainer Martens) arranged under headings such as "youth sports", how to coach children and young people, physical conditioning, improving skills, and treatment and prevention of injuries.

Coaching Focus
Issue 2, Autumn 1985

16 pp.   ISSN 0267-4416   50 pence

(Available from the National Coaching Foundation, 4 College Close, Beckett Park, Leeds LS6 3QH.)

Special issue on "Competitive Sport and Young Children".